3 STRATEGIES FOR EARNING ON CRYPTOCURRENCY

HOW TO CREATE A STABLE AND LONG-TERM BUSINESS USING THE GROWING TREND.

Your Gift

I wanted to show my appreciation that you support my work so I've put together a free gift for you.

http://bonusfreebook.org/

Just visit the link above to download it now.

I know you will love this gift.

If you like this book, you can see and buy my other books on this link:

Thank you for attention!

With love,

Adam Clark

INTRODUCTION

CRYPTOCURRENCY - WHAT ARE YOU?

HISTORY OF CRYPTOCURRENCY

Virtual currency has always been offered by merchants and businesses for a long time now and it served as a token to represent fiat money. This virtual currency could also be used to make all the payments, it could be transferred to individuals and it could be saved in form of credits. This idea was conceived as far back as in the 1980s. The objective of creating such an outstanding and significant idea was to provide a solution to the challenges that befell the fiat money.

TECHNICAL FOUNDATIONS

David Chaum, an American cryptographer was the first to create the first internet money called DigiCash in his native country, the Netherlands. This invention gained massive media attention to the extent that Microsoft made an offer of $180 million to Chaum to install DigiCash on all Windows PC around the globe but due to some technical blunders, that was not efficiently carried out and it led to the eventual bankruptcy of the Central Bank of Netherlands in the year of 1998. As a result of the failures in the past, another wave of internet money came into existence. A solution to payment issues was made available by startups alongside a virtual money system with some tweaks everywhere. However, Paypal became the winner because it understood clearly what the users' needs were. Paypal provided a coherent peer-to-peer transfer medium alongside an easy way of allowing payments for these merchants.

The most remarkable digital currency of the late 1990s and 2000s in the United States was 'e-gold'. The e-gold was designed by a company in Florida with the same name 'E-gold'. The company, E-gold, functioned basically as a buyer of digital gold. Trinkets, old jewelry, and coins were sent to the company's warehouse by the company's customers while they received virtual "e-gold" in the form of ounces of gold. E-gold customers then traded their earnings to other customers, withdrew their holdings in exchange for physical gold or fiat money. E-gold got to its peak around the mid-2000s having millions of accounts and processing billions annually. However, as a result of poor security encryption, it became a victim of a hack attack and subsequently, it lost a lot of its funds and stripped its customers of their investments. As of 2009, the platform was closed down on the back of insurmountable legal pressure that resulted from its attractive compliance policies which money launderers capitalized on and also Ponzi schemes and as such, it was labeled legally dubious. The USA's economic crisis in 2008 began to be a checkpoint in the history of the global economy as it exposed the dangerous practices of financial experts all around the world. Satoshi Nakamoto, an unknown entity, published a whitepaper around 2009 to explain the concept of blockchain alongside its technology and the source code. He also created the first cryptocurrency called Bitcoin. Nakamoto successfully created the Bitcoin and released it to the public in the early 2009. Some very enthusiastic individuals began exchanging and mining this virtual currency. Bitcoin and blockchain technology gave rise to other cryptocurrencies as a result of the public interest in them. Currently, more than 850 cryptocurrencies exist with Dash, Litecoin, Ripple, Monero, and others being the most popular ones. As of June 2017, the market value of all cryptocurrencies put together is about $100 billion which indeed is a landmark achievement in the crypto-journey. The WordPress is recorded to be the first merchant to trade using Bitcoin in late 2012. Newegg.com, Expedia, Microsoft, and others followed the suit. Today, a lot of merchants indulge in the use of the worlds' most known cryptocurrencies as a legitimate mode of payment. At the same time, some other crypto-coins are accepted widely for payments too. Also, these altcoins could be exchanged for either Bitcoin or fiat money which helps providing flexibility and high liquidity.

Satoshi Nakamoto's 2008 whitepaper started a revolution. At that time, only technology enthusiasts understood the potential that blockchain technology offered the market. With time, more people have gotten a good grasp of the potential that this groundbreaking technology has to offer. As a result, 2017 has been the year when the market has truly taken off. The price of Bitcoin jumped to around 85,000, and it is expected to continue rising for the foreseeable future. Even other altcoins like Ripple, Ethereum, and Dash, have experienced an exponential increase in value. The reason why cryptocurrencies and blockchain technology are gaining popularity is mainly due to the superiority it has over other similar platforms. It excels in three main categories and they are as follows:

First, it is decentralized, unlike most other financial systems that rely on a central body. This eliminates the risk of internal fraud since the users truly own the platforms or cryptocurrencies. Everyone has the entire list of the transactions, and any changes will be visible to everyone.

Second is the anonymity it offers to the users. Blockchain technology uses both encryption and pseudonyms to ensure that sensitive user information is kept away from the prying eyes of nefarious individuals. This makes it a suitable replacement for payment transfer and e-commerce that is normally attacked by phishers who are willing to obtain the sensitive user information.

Lastly, blockchain technology offers unparalleled security. The ledger that stores the information is decentralized and the information is synchronized on all devices. In the centralized platforms, hackers need only attack the servers housing the information with either ransom ware or DDoS attacks. However, the shared computational power of blockchain makes it impossible. Bitcoin alone has the computational power of over 100 supercomputers.

These three factors have endeared cryptocurrencies to their enthusiasts. They are safe and secure for every user. Within the next few years, cryptocurrencies may become popular enough for mainstream adoptions. In a new light, in a new era

BACKGROUND

As more people become blockchain enthusiasts, the cryptocurrency market continues to grow. According to Google, the interest in the term Bitcoin has grown to an all-time record high. The hype and buzz about the cryptocurrency industry keeps growing as more people try to understand this market. This increase in interest has boosted the investor participation in the market. Even investors, who were not interested in cryptocurrency in the past, are now turning to it as an alternative income generator. As a result, the capitalization of the market has grown substantially. In 2017 alone, the market capitalization has grown from $17.7 billion to over $255 billion as of November. This represents a 1,204 percent increase in market capitalization that is sure to draw the attention of any serious investor.

The market gives investors multiple ways to earn revenues. The first is through mining. This involves the creation of mining rigs that earn digital currencies by contributing to the creation of transaction blocks. The earnings are just a few cents made per transaction block but if this amount is converted to USD based on the 1BTC = 5,000 USD, the earnings are quite handsome. The second method used in investing relies on investing in cryptocurrency startups. This is a risky strategy but considering there is someone who bought ETH at $1 and now it has risen to over $250, it is an exponential increase in profits. However, the most common method of making money in the cryptocurrency industry is through speculative trading. Purchasing cryptocurrencies at a low price and selling them at a slightly higher price. This is somewhat similar to FX trading only that the assets being traded are cryptocurrencies.

THE UNTAPPED INVESTMENT OPPORTUNITIES

Cryptocurrency trading is a lucrative investment opportunity for all savvy investors. Three factors make it a good investment option. First, there is less liquidity in the industry. The cryptocurrency industry is not as liquid as the FX market. As a result, it is subject to drastic fluctuations when some high-volume orders are placed. This creates an opportunity for investors to make substantial money when the difference between the buying price and selling price is big.

Second, the cryptocurrency industry is quite volatile. Prices are always rising and falling depending on the market changes. This makes it the perfect market for the speculative investors. Whenever a cryptocurrency falls, investors can purchase the coins only to sell them off when the value rises. The drastic difference in prices makes this the best investment option for the most.

The final alternative is making money by leveraging the price differences that exist in cryptocurrency exchanges. Unlike the FX market, which is subject to a lot of stringent regulations to ensure that currency prices are stable in all the markets, the cryptocurrency market is largely unregulated. As a result, there are substantial differences in the buying and selling prices of different exchanges. Investors can leverage these differences to make significant profits. Even though the margins are not that big, a large number of trades can prove lucrative. This is an untapped opportunity that few investors have been able to maximize.

Chapter 1
POPULAR VIRTUAL CRYPTOCURRENCIES

Cryptocurrency is a virtual or digital currency that makes use of cryptography for encryption to verify transactions, to secure the information concerning the transactions, and to make money. Cryptocurrency makes use of a decentralized system as opposed to the fiat money and electronic money which operate on a centralized system. The decentralized nature of every cryptocurrency is so because it is built on the blockchain technology. The blockchain technology is more like a database for public transactions and also functions as a ledger. Cryptocurrency is a system that allows online users to process transactions with the use of an exchange unit called virtual currency. This virtual currency is also referred to as the virtual money; it is a type of unregulated and distributed money that is controlled by its developer. At the same time, cryptocurrencies can either be centralized or decentralized, meaning that the money supply is controlled from a central point or that the money supply is controlled from numerous sources. The control of each cryptocurrency comes from the blockchain that serves as a public ledger for all the cryptocurrency transactions.

According to Lansky Jan, every cryptocurrency must have the following characteristics:
- It must be independent, not requiring a centralized authority
- It must be able to keep an overview of a crypto unit and the owners of these units
- It should define the possibility of creating new crypto units, define the means and determine the owner of the unit as well
- Ownership of these units should be verifiable exclusively through cryptography

Furthermore, cryptocurrency is a form of digital money that is designed to be used for instantaneous transactions that are based on cryptographic principles.

BITCOIN

Bitcoin happens to be the first decentralized and the most recognized cryptocurrency payment system. It was released as an open-source software to reward the process of mining in 2009. But before then, it was first mentioned in a whitepaper that was published on October 31, 2008. Bitcoin is designed in such an independent way that it does not require the need to store or move the money to the banks. Impressively, bitcoins possess trade value like they do in the physical market realm.

The longer it stays, the more valuable it becomes, and it can be used to purchase goods online.

Swiftcoin (BitSwift)

Daniel Bruno founded Swiftcoin in 2011 with a number of admirable features. Particularly, Swiftcoin was the first to support currency creation by interest paid on debts including a theoretical value based on the work required to produce electricity. In the same fashion as Bitcoin, it is also not dependent on any web-site or bank. One of the unique features of Swiftcoin is its ability to support encrypted mails with attachments and its anonymity. This is an alternative to bitcoin as it makes use of similar blockchain technology. However, Swiftcoin differs from Bitcoin in the absence of mining opportunities.

LITECOIN

Just like bitcoin, Litecoin was released through an open source on October 7, 2011 by Charlie Lee but went live on October 13, 2011. When it comes to mining, Litecoin has a fixed supply which is 84 million Litecoin units. Moreover, Litecoin provides incentives for the first-time miners who would successfully verify a block with 50 Litecoins. Also, in order to reduce the fear of overproduction in people, Litecoin is designed to restrict the number of units in circulation. This is simply because it would be difficult for the new currency to develop a reputation in the market place. Creating and transferring coins is managed not by a central authority but rather by an open source cryptographic protocol. It is different from Bitcoin in the sense that it processes a block in every 2.5minutes as opposed to Bitcoin's time of 10minutes. It also makes use of scripts in its proof-of-work algorithm.

PEER COIN

Scott Nadal and Sunny King are said to be the authors of this platform, although Sunny King is a pseudonym. It got its inspiration from Bitcoin as it shares its source code and also its technical implementation. Peercoin is the first peer-to-peer cryptocurrency to use the POW and POS functions and was conceptualized in 2013. Peercoin yields an unlimited number of coins because it is designed to experience a steady 1% inflation per year. Equally important to note is the proof of stake in Peercoin that requires minimal emerging consumption in generating coins. This staking process collects nodes based on that they are being held in an individual's virtual wallet. The creation of coin could either be through mining or minting. In comparison to Bitcoin, Peer coin is different as a result of its emphasis on a hybrid approach to mining.

PRIME COIN

Primecoin is created by an anonymous person or group known as Sunny King who is also in charge of Peercoin. These two cryptocurrencies share a lot of similarities. There are special prime-number chains known as Cunningham chains and bi-twin chains, it is exactly the prime number chains that the prime network searches for. In Primecoin, the adaptation by the mining community is the determinant of the number of Primecoin units that will be mined. Therefore, instead of having hard-set ultimate number coins, Prime coin released per block is always equal to 999 divided by the square of difficulty.

ETHEREUM

Vitalik Buterinis the author of the Ethereum cryptocurrency. Ether is another name for ethereum and its blockchain is maintained by the ethereum ledger that provides a distributed ledger for the transactions. Unlike Bitcoin's blockchain, Ethereum blockchain is focused on running the program code of any decentralized application, rather than being used to track digital currency ownership. In actual sense, Ethereum is a type of crypto-token that is used to fuel the network. So, instead of miners to be mining for Bitcoin, they mine to earn ether in Ethereum block chain. In addition, ethereum also allows developers to create whatever operations that they want.

TITCOIN

Titcoin is peculiar for its usage of pornography to manage the issuance of new currency units while processing transactions on a decentralized peer-to-peer networking. Founded by 3 people, Edward Mansfield, Richard Allen and the third anonymous person, it was, however, the first cryptocurrency to be nominated for a major industry award covered by a variety of mainstream news outlets. Since its inception in January 2014, Titcoin has been dedicated to promoting and marketing Titcoin to the customers across various adult products and services. It shares source code with Bitcoin, however, with major modifications to the system software helping to increase transaction speed and readjusting the difficulty that plagues network. It has a total coin supply of 69million and a block time of 1 min.

RIPPLE

Ripple, also called the 'Ripple Transaction Protocol' and is quite distinct and complex if compared to other cryptocurrencies. This is because, Ripple is a real-time gross settlement, currency exchange and remittance system. In short, Ripple network does not run with a proof of work nor with a proof of a stake system. However, banks and payment networks have adopted Ripple as a settlement infrastructure technology.

Chapter 2
Magic strategies

Mining

The cryptocurrency industry provides a platform for investors to generate income in different ways. One of such ways is through mining. Mining cryptocurrencies is a really rewarding system most especially for early users. For example, when a crypto coin hits the mainstream to become a global phenomenon, it attracts the interest of new investors. However, the production of crypto-coins is not a simple process like fiat money as it operates without any central authority whatsoever. Hence, there is usually a need to generate more coins and it is done through the process of mining.

First of all, you need to understand what blockchain is before you can understand how mining works. Blockchain is a technology, which almost all the cryptocurrencies are built on. It is characteristically created to operate on a decentralized system with a public ledger which shows every transaction that has ever been conducted within a given cryptocurrency. These transactions are collected into what is called 'blocks'. These blocks would then be verified to determine if legitimate by individuals called 'miners'. The miners ensure that the coin has not been spent before. They also make sure that the amount of input and output match. At this point, next transaction block is linked to it. This basically is how miners act, how the cryptocurrencies are created and also how new units are generated. Any individual can make money by mining new blocks. The idea is since there is no central authority, any individual has to be in charge of collating all transactions performed so as to form a new block. Any time a transaction is collated into a block, it is added into the blockchain and whenever these blocks are assembled by an individual, such individual is rewarded with units of coins. However, to avoid the devaluation of the currency by miners through the creation of large volumes of new blocks, creating a block therefore is made more difficult and artificial through solving very complex math problem called 'proof of work'

Also, by calculating a hash, one can earn a lot of money. In creating a block, a cryptographic hash should always be attached as it is needed in fulfilling some requirements. There is only one realistic way to make a hash match the right criteria and that is by calculating as many as one can do and waiting till one gets the matching hash. Once the right hash is discovered, a new block would be created. The miner who found the right hash would be rewarded with units of coins. It is more like a competition where you get to guess with an added advantage of having multiple opportunities to guess. The first person to give the correct answer earns the reward. The faster you are at providing the answer, the more reward you get. As lucrative as this might be, there are limits of which one can earn. Miners are always competing against one another so as to calculate as many hashes as they can to earn more. However, there is usually a difficulty level when it comes to calculating hashes as a new block is usually harder to mine than the previous one.

This, therefore, ensures that the creation of new blocks remains steady. Also, a lot of cryptocoins tend to have a finite number of units to be generated at all. For instance, there are only 21 million Bitcoins to be created in the world. Once it gets to the limit, it is impossible to generate any other Bitcoin. In addition, Cryptocurrency mining is subject to certain requirements as it is rare for an individual to mine with a computer which used to be the case before. As miners increase in number, the requirement becomes stiffer. For instance, it used to be a processor that is moderately powerful, after that it became a high-end GPU, then different GPU working together, and now, it's a special chip that is designed basically for mining.

In summary, digital currencies are earned through the contribution to the formation of transaction blocks. Although the earnings acquired per transaction block seem to be a few cents, they worth something good when converted to USD based on the 1BTC = 5,000 USD

Trading

Another means through which one can earn on cryptocurrency is by becoming a cryptocurrency trader. A trader is a person who is engaged in buying and selling of goods and services. Typically, a cryptocurrency trader is one who carries out the buying and selling of Cryptocurrencies. The potential for making a lot of money in trading cryptocurrencies is usually pretty tremendous especially when you have good business acumen and more so, such individual should have a certain level of expertise in the market and must also be knowledgeable about how this works in general, just as it is demanded in every other market or financial platform. The fundamental fact is that cryptocurrencies rely on exchanges I.e.

Buying and selling, same way the fiat currency does. However, there are more similarities when compared to the stock market. This is so because both the stock market and cryptocurrency market are erratic. i.e., they are really unstable which could frequently make one feel it's too much of a risk to take. For instance, just of recent, there was a massive decrease in the value of cryptocurrencies all around the world. Basically, it takes a lot of courage to stay in observing the market and it takes much more courage to keep investing in spite of the situation. Selling and buying in the crypto market is very similar to the trade in the penny stock trading. This trade is prone to a lot of fluctuations but you can earn a lot of money in this market, all you need to do is to be very alert and aware of the various trends. Also, you need to be well-equipped with the right decisions through qualitative research as it would help you know the risks that come paired with trading.

There are thousands of cryptocurrencies on the crypto market. However, most of them are created just for profit sake only to go into extinction after fulfilling its goal. So, this is the reason why you have to be up and going, especially in regards to the latest crypto news so as to know the latest buzz about a particular coin. If the buzz is about the potential fall, you would be able to discharge it in order to avoid any loss of profits. On the other hand, choosing to hold on to the cryptocurrencies may seem great, however, it is not very much advisable except when dealing with Bitcoin or Ethereum as they have a seemingly lasting potential.

Basically, trading involves exchanging dollars or whatsoever fiat for digital money. Just like the stock market, you buy a coin and let it grow in value; you can later then sell it for much more than you bought it, although, that is dependent on the timing and strategy. However, when you are ready to cash out, just do if it's worth it. More graphically, if you spent a

$1,000 on acquiring Ether let's say as of March 2017, for the price of $25 per coin, that's 40 coins in total. The worth of that coin today would be around $269 per coin, bringing about a geometric increase in value from $1,000 to $10,760. To make profit, one would have to convert the coin to cash.

Cryptocurrency Exchanges

The most known place where buying and trading of cryptocurrency take place is the exchanges. They are certain places where buying and selling of crypto can be done through fiat money. There are various measures for estimating the quality and reliability of an exchange, like spread, liquidity, purchase, withdrawal limits, fees, security, user friendliness, insurance and trading volume etc. One of the best exchanges with a beginner-friendly interface and a high-quality crypto-insurance is the Coinbase. It is so simple that you just need to setup your account, add your bank account details and verify the details. Here are the five very simple steps to start trading:

1. Select the 'Buy/Sell coin' icon
2. Choose the payment method by using the drop-down menu
3. Insert the amount you want to trade
4. Select 'buy coin' instantly
5. Go to your dashboard to view your crypto balance

Once you know how to buy cryptocurrency, you'd be naturally willing to try crypto trading, for example, BTC/ETH. All you have to do is to make a transfer from your Coinbase account to GDAX for free in order to begin trading. Coinbase is more like a platform where crypto coins can be stored conveniently and also a place to buy your crypto coins while GDAX is a platform for margin trading. In spite of all the latter, the transfer is strictly free and also instantaneous. As you slowly get familiar with other currencies, you might want to have the option of investing in them. Polo and Bitter are also the exchanges where trade can take place.

Always make sure you verify your account details and submit the requested documents in time so as to avoid getting involved in any problem whatsoever when a lucrative deal is lurking around. Verification could be strenuous although as it could take few days. More so, withdrawal and purchase limits also get to increase as trading increases. In addition, when using any fiat currency other than USD, endeavor to check out the exchange rates for withdrawal and funding so as to avoid withdrawal problems during the exchange. There is a reoccurring scam, known as the "pump-and-dump". This is when an investor buys a lot of crypto coins only to inflate the price. Once it reaches the peak, the latter individual sells all his assets bringing a fall in the price. The crypto moguls must keep an eye on the situations like this so as to keep a safe slate.

Anyway, in the cryptocurrency industry, the most common way to make money is through speculative trading. It involves buying cryptocurrencies at a low price and selling them at a bit higher price.

Freelancing

Freelancing is the act of performing one's duty outside of the chain of command and the standard of procedure. Freelancing is becoming a very common thing in the world of today. According to The Freelancer's union, there are about 42 million freelancers in the United States and based on some predictions, by 2020, they would occupy half of the labor force. Due to the wide range of possibilities provided by the blockchain and cryptocurrency invention, freelancing would most likely to double up in the next few years. Cryptocurrency is becoming a wide-spread phenomenon all around the globe.

According to Wikipedia, as of 7th of January, 2018, there are over 1384 cryptocurrencies all around the world and the market is still growing. It means that another cryptocurrency can be created at any point in time. In creating a cryptocurrency, there are a lot of things involved as a result of the intricacies comprised the in cryptocurrency itself. From creating to marketing ICO to maintaining, there are things to be put in place. As a freelance writer, for instance, you could serve in the writing sector by providing the articles for public awareness, whitepaper to explain how the coin is going to work and how the ICO would go. Upon providing this service, the freelance writer would be paid with the coin in question. Now it is necessary that the freelancer is smart enough to determine if the cryptocurrency in question is perspective enough to make it through the market and also to remain in the market. For instance, if at the beginning of the creation of Bitcoin a freelancer helps with the writing of the whitepaper, such individual would be paid in Bitcoins and fortunately, Bitcoin is the major cryptocurrency in the world today, and the latter individual could become very rich if he sells his coins right now. It is worthy to note that this is not limited to writers alone.

Also, as a freelancer, one can decide to work for an established cryptocurrency, providing his service in exchange for payment in cryptocurrencies. Although, this is not limited to crypto-companies but also can be used by any company that can make payments in cryptocurrencies. Thus, you can work for someone or some people and get paid in cryptocurrency. There is usually no limit to which one can earn cryptocurrency as a freelancer. Today, there are many freelancing platforms created by cryptocurrencies towards solving the shortcomings witnessed in the freelancing platforms in which fiat money is the mode of exchange. Freelancers, therefore, go to this marketplace to sell their services and get paid in cryptocurrency upon the completion of the task. The Freelancer can then sell the coin for fiat money or store it for a while till it grows in value and then sell it for more than he actually charged for his service.

There is a need for a lot of thinking and planning to make use of this strategy. This strategy also relies on the extensive knowledge of the crypto-market so as to make out the best deal from it. One major difference between the first two strategies and freelancing is the fact that freelancing provides services to earn cryptocurrency while the first ones involve spending of fiat money to acquire machines for mining and cryptocurrency for trading.

Conclusion

It is no longer new that cryptocurrencies have a lot of opportunities to offer. The same way it has changed the financial world is the same way it aims to change the earning pattern and worth of humans. There are just numerous benefits which cryptocurrencies are to provide. The three strategies listed and explained above are very practical strategies through which an individual can make earnings. Trading, mining and freelancing are the real sources of money, however, they have their weaknesses and strongholds. One has to be skillful enough to invest to make earnings through any of the above strategies.

Your Gift

I wanted to show my appreciation that you support my work so I've put together a free gift for you.

http://bonusfreebook.org/

Just visit the link above to download it now.

I know you will love this gift.

If you like this book, you can see and buy my other books on this link:

Thank you for attention!

With love,

Adam Clark

To our customers we give a discount of $10,

it's very easy to get it, use the coupon code

on the link

HERE

Text Copyright 2018 © Adam Clark

All rights reserved. No part of this guide may be reproduced in any form without permission in writing from the publisher except in the case of brief quotations embodied in critical articles or reviews.

Legal & Disclaimer

The information contained in this book and its contents is not designed to replace or take the place of any form of medical or professional advice; and is not meant to replace the need for independent medical, financial, legal or other professional advice or services, as may be required. The content and information in this book have been provided for educational and entertainment purposes only.

The content and information contained in this book have been compiled from sources deemed reliable, and it is accurate to the best of the Author's knowledge, information and belief. However, the Author cannot guarantee its accuracy and validity and cannot be held liable for any errors and/or omissions. Further, changes are periodically made to this book as and when needed. Where appropriate and/or necessary, you must consult a professional (including but not limited to your doctor, attorney, financial advisor or such other professional advisor) before using any of the suggested remedies, techniques, or information in this book.

Upon using the contents and information contained in this book, you agree to hold harmless the Author from and against any damages, costs, and expenses, including any legal fees potentially resulting from the application of any of the information provided by this book. This disclaimer applies to any loss, damages or injury caused by the use and application, whether directly or indirectly, of any advice or information presented, whether for breach of contract, tort, negligence, personal injury, criminal intent, or under any other cause of action.

You agree to accept all risks of using the information presented in this book.

You agree that by continuing to read this book, where appropriate and/or necessary, you shall consult a professional (including but not limited to your doctor, attorney, or financial advisor or such other advisor as needed) before using any of the suggested remedies, techniques, or information in this book.

www.ingramcontent.com/pod-product-compliance
Lightning Source LLC
Chambersburg PA
CBHW062237220526
45471CB00009B/3518